KU-671-265

THE SACRIFICE OF CHRIST

By the same Author:

AN IDIOM BOOK OF NEW TESTAMENT GREEK

THE MEANING OF HOPE

C. F. D. MOULE

Fellow of Clare College
Lady Margaret's Professor of Divinity in the University of Cambridge

THE

SACRIFICE OF

CHRIST

LONDON
HODDER AND STOUGHTON

First Printed 1956

MADE AND PRINTED IN GREAT BRITAIN FOR
HODDER AND STOUGHTON LIMITED, LONDON
BY C. TINLING AND CO., LTD., LIVERPOOL, LONDON
AND PRESCOT

CONTENTS

ACKNOWLEDGMENTS

All quotations in this book are included with the kind permission of the following authors and publishers to whom we acknowledge our indebtedness and wish to express our thanks:

For the extract from *Peter Abelard* by Helen Waddell, published by Messrs. Constable & Co. Ltd.

For a review of *The Fulness of Christ* by Canon Alan Richardson, which appeared in "The Churchman," in June 1951.

For two extracts from *The Shape of the Liturgy* by Dom Gregory Dix, published by the Dacre Press.

For two extracts from *Christus Veritas* by William Temple, published by Macmillan & Co. Ltd., and included by the kind permission of Mrs. Temple.

For a review by the Reverend R. C. Walls which appeared in *The Cambridge Review*, Vol. lxxvi.

For Fr. Hebert's article from *Ways of Worship*, published by the Student Christian Movement Press Ltd.

FOREWORD

In launching this slight essay on the sea of however small
a group of readers, I am very well aware that I am courting
shipwreck on the rocks of scholarly criticism if not on some
others of an even sharper kind. The informal lectures, of
which it still virtually consists (for they have been only very
slightly touched up) were originally delivered to a friendly
group of ordinands.* And the only excuses for sending them
further afield are two: the first, that some of the original
hearers were kind enough to suggest it and the Publishers
most kindly furthered the project; and the second, that the
present time seems favourable, as I have said in the
lectures, for the ventilating of the subject. Perhaps never
before has there been so much mutual understanding—
or at least desire for it—between the different traditions
of the Christian Church. I cannot resist quoting from
Fr. Hebert to illustrate this. The following words (cited
by Dr. Massey H. Shepherd in the Minneapolis addresses)
would only need to be very slightly altered, near the middle
of the quotation, to serve as a summary of what I try to
say in these talks:

> "The eucharistic Sacrifice, that storm-centre of controversy,
> is finding in our day a truly evangelical expression from the
> 'catholic' side, when it is insisted that the sacrificial action
> is not any sort of re-immolation of Christ, nor a sacrifice
> additional to His one Sacrifice, but a participation in it. The
> true celebrant is Christ the High-Priest, and the Christian

* They were the Holy Week Lectures at Cuddesdon College in 1955,
by kind invitation of the Principal. I owe very warm thanks to him,
his Staff, and his men for their kindly welcome.

people are assembled as members of His Body to present before God His Sacrifice, and to be themselves offered up in sacrifice through their union with Him. This, however, involves a repudiation of certain mediaeval developments, notably the habitual celebration of the Eucharist without the Communion of the people; or the notion that the offering of the Eucharist is the concern of the individual priest rather than of the assembled church; and, above all, any idea that in the Eucharist we offer a sacrifice to propitiate God. We offer it only because He has offered the one Sacrifice, once for all, in which we need to participate" (from *Ways of Worship*, S.C.M. 1951).

It may be, then, that even so ephemeral and tentative a discussion as this may prove to be some small contribution to the healing of our divisions: a little tract for the times.

It is only one individual trying to think aloud about a perennial problem. And to any who are patient enough to listen, he wishes to say two more things before he begins. First, pride bids me anticipate criticism by saying that, if there is any realm in which I can claim some experience, it is in biblical exposition. Outside it—and especially in the disciplines of philosophy, history, and liturgy (where much of the following discussion lies)—I am the merest amateur and pretend to be no more. My justification, if any, for trespassing has already been offered. Secondly, anxiety for goodwill compels me to say also that I hope that those Evangelicals with whom I have joined issue will be ready to believe that, in regard to essentials, I am with them still. If we must use labels, I am proud to call myself an Evangelical.

C. F. D. MOULE

I

INTRODUCTORY

THE subject which is offered for discussion in these chapters is a familiar one, but so great and deep a mystery that we can hardly think about it too often. It is the strange paradox which lies at the very heart of our faith, and which arises from the finality and yet constantly repetitive nature of salvation—the finished work of God in Christ, over against his continued work in the Body of Christ which is the Church. It is the tension set up by the distinction, yet union, between Christ as an individual and the corporate Christ in his Church. It is the restless question of the relation between the sacrifice on Calvary and (as some would put it) "the sacrifice of the Mass". Imagine somebody who has little or no theological background, but who is a really serious enquirer into the Christian faith. Suppose that, in studying his New Testament, he encounters these two strands of its texture in quick succession. First he reads the cry of finality and achievement, the τετέλεσται—"It is finished"—in the Fourth Gospel's story of the Cross. Or he reads these equally absolute phrases in the Epistle to the Hebrews: Christ "has no need, like those high priests, to offer sacrifices daily, first for his own sins and then for those of the people; he did this *once for all* when he offered up himself" (7^{27}); or: "Nor was it to offer himself repeatedly, as the high priest enters the Holy Place yearly with blood not his own; for then he would have had to suffer repeatedly since the foundation of the world. But as it is, he has appeared *once for all* at the end of the age to put away sin by the sacrifice of himself" ($9^{25f.}$, R.S.V.). And then our enquirer, having done his best to grasp and come to terms with this "scandal of particularity", this astonishing claim that the eternal and final and absolute is in some sense fastened at a moment in the flux of time, goes on to find himself after all confronted with the famous words of St. Paul in Col. 1[24] about the continuation and completion of the work of salvation in the Christian Church: ". . . who now rejoice in my sufferings for you, and fill up that which is behind of the afflictions of Christ in my flesh, for his body's sake, which is the Church". What would you say to such a person if he asked you in perplexity just what this meant? It is not easy to give a fair answer; and too often the answers stated or implied are lopsided. And this brings us at once to frankly controversial territory.

The Protestant tends to stress the "once for all", the ἅπαξ, clinging resolutely to the precious good news that salvation is complete and Christ's finished work sufficient. The Roman Church, while wholeheartedly acknowledging this, would also (I think it is true to say) stress the frequentative and the repetitive aspects of salvation. Similarly, the Protestant emphasis falls upon the uniqueness of Christ and his historical past, while the opposite wing, again accepting all that, will pay more attention to the Church as the Body of Christ contemporary with every age—the continuation of his presence. Arising in part from these contrasts is another pair of antitheses: it is notorious that on the whole the Protestant tends to individualism in religion (though many qualifications need to be added to that rash generalisation), while the opposite emphasis is upon its corporate nature. Eucharistic doctrine naturally follows the same main divide, and that in many respects; but the most obvious is the matter of sacrifice. At one end of thought, the act of offering is relegated—or appears to the outside observer to be relegated—to a secondary or lower position, while representatives of the opposite end may not stop short of speaking of the offering of Christ at each Mass; or, at the very least, thinkers on that side of the divide will wish to bring the act of offering up into a position of prominence. The position of the Prayer of Oblation in the 1662 Prayer Book is often interpreted as standing for the Protestant emphasis—the reluctance to associate the idea of offering with the main action of the service, and the preference for mentioning it only as a consequence, not as a part, of the sacrament itself.

I take some examples of these different stresses in Eucharistic thought and practice from some recent comparatively incidental writings. First from *The Fulness of Christ*.* This, it will be remembered, was the Evangelical Anglican member of that trilogy of replies to certain questions formulated by the Archbishop of Canterbury, the other members of which were *Catholicity*,† from the opposite side of Anglicanism, and *The Catholicity of Protestantism*,‡ from the Free Churches. In *The Fulness of Christ* (p. 32) came these words about the Eucharistic offering: "The Eucharist is the divinely instituted remembrance of Christ's sacrifice, and in it God gives and the Church receives the fruits of that sacrifice, the Body and Blood of Christ. In virtue of this, and only so, the Church is enabled to make that offering of praise, thanksgiving, and self-oblation which (apart from the alms) is the only sacrifice actually offered in the Eucharist. Only as united to Christ in his death and resurrection through receiving the Body and Blood of Christ is the Church able to offer itself acceptably to the Father".

Canon Alan Richardson, in a review§ which in the main was very friendly and appreciative, took up this point vigorously when he wrote:

In implying . . . that the bread and wine are *not* offered in

* S.P.C.K., 1950.   † Dacre Press, 1947.   ‡ Lutterworth Press, 1950.
§ In *The Churchman*, June 1951.

B

the Eucharist, they deny the primitive (second-century) conception of the Eucharist as a sacrament of Creation as well as of Redemption, through the offering up of the "first-fruits" of the created order under the forms of bread and wine. In the early Church every Lord's Day was a Harvest Festival as well as an Easter Sunday. Furthermore, they deny the primitive symbolism of the offering of the sacramental elements as representing the worshippers themselves—"There you are on the altar, there you are in the chalice", said St. Augustine to his congregation at the Eucharist. They destroy the whole symbolism of the "People's Offering", now so widely practised in Anglican churches, with the precious note of realism which it introduces into the liturgy as the worshippers come to offer to God not only themselves but all the labours of their hands, represented under the forms of manufactured articles, the bread and wine of the eucharistic offering. There is lacking the sense of grandeur and mystery in the eucharistic oblation, which Christ, true priest at every celebration, offers to God as He presents His body the Church already—eschatologically—made pure and spotless, a living sacrifice, holy, acceptable to God. But the Church (*Laos*) is one with Christ as Offerer as well as with him as offered; the priesthood of the *Laos* derives from the eternal high priesthood of Christ.

I must be allowed to say in parenthesis, as one of the signatories to *The Fulness of Christ*, that I am sure that none of us in fact intended to "deny the primitive symbolism of the offering of the sacramental elements as representing the worshippers themselves", still less to "destroy the whole symbolism of 'the People's Offering'" (a symbolism in which I for one habitually join with the greatest of profit). But it is perfectly true that the two emphases—one on receiving and the other on giving—do serve as symptoms of a difference. Here, next,* are a couple of instances of an extreme anti-sacrificial position from Anglican writers of the Evangelical school (a position

---

* *The Churchman*, Dec. 1954, pp. 233f., 255.

which I, though proud to be of that school, cannot myself accept unqualified). One writer says "The Atonement is something wholly other than ourselves. We have nothing to add to the Atonement, nor can we add anything to the Sacrifice of Christ upon the Cross, *least of all by joining in His self-offering*". Another in a review repudiates "all views that suggest that the eternal Son of God is continually offering Himself in order to secure our acceptance with God". Returning back from this to illustrate the opposite stress, here is a very important observation made by my friend Mr. Roland Walls of Corpus Christi College, Cambridge. In Clare College Chapel, Dr. Robinson, the Dean, has introduced in a very impressive form the People's Offering (which I said just now I had myself found so profitable), and several other similar features, embodying them in a manual which is aimed at helping the worshipper to participate, not as an isolated individual, but as an active member of the community. Reviewing this manual most appreciatively,* Mr. Walls adds: "This book leaves one thing unsaid or unstressed and that is the age-old belief of Christians that in the Holy Communion the family of God have an opportunity of joining in and pleading the offering to the Father of the one perfect sacrifice of the Son of God. Something like the words of William Bright's hymn, now to be found in the hymnbooks of free-church and presbyterian traditions, needs to be given on the left-hand page [that is, the part of the manual devoted to comments and aids to prayer]:—

> And now, O Father, mindful of the love
> That bought us once for all on Calvary's tree,
> And having with us Him who pleads above,
> We here present, we here spread forth to Thee
> That only offering perfect in Thine eyes,
> The one true, pure, immortal sacrifice."

* In *The Cambridge Review*, vol. lxxvi (Oct., 1954–June, 1955), p. 316.

For the moment I make no comment on this: we shall have occasion to return to it. But I have simply quoted these varying viewpoints in quick succession, taken not from considered works of doctrine such as Dr. Mascall's *Corpus Christi*, or, before him, Gore's *The Body of Christ*, but from current and comparatively incidental and ephemeral writings, just in order to remind ourselves of the welter of opinion, even about this one question of the eucharistic sacrifice, let alone the related problems.

Where different branches of the Church advance opposite views or stress opposite ends of a series, there is generally something precious in both insights. And it is not so much the mean between the two that we must seek, as the common root from which these two different growths shoot up; and it is my belief moreover that in this particular instance there is real hope of common ground being discovered by our both being willing (if one may press the metaphor a little further) to dig down deeper than we generally do towards that root. I have been particularly impressed over the last few years by the richness of the unity that I have been able to find at the deeper levels of this controversy, both in the reviewing of Roman Catholic works on the New Testament, and in discussions, and in common worship with Christians of varying standpoints.

It is for this reason that I venture to offer these informal talks about the Sacrifice of Christ, believing that if they lead us to study together in the context of worship the Gospel of Salvation which we hold in common, we shall, by God's grace, have taken a not unimportant step forward into that mutual understanding from which God can build a stronger and more united church. In the three chapters which follow, therefore, I shall ask you to consider first, the uniqueness and finality of the sacrifice of Christ and all the precious truth which has been guarded with especial care by the Protestant emphasis on the once-and-for-all security of our salvation. This is the ground of all Christian confidence: the objective, finished work of Christ —achieved, unalterable. Secondly (that is, in the third chapter) we shall come to the correlative truth contained in the New Testament phrases of repetition ("I fill up that which is lacking of the afflictions of Christ") and is implicit in the doctrine of the coinherence of believers and Christ. The doctrine of the Church as the Body of Christ carries in it the corollary that in some sense the sufferings of the limbs are the sufferings of the Head, and vice versa. Finally, in the last chapter, we shall try to think about the implications of all this for eucharistic doctrine.

If some suggestions may be allowed by way of pointers to appropriate reading and thinking in this connection, first, the Epistle to the Hebrews, which is one of the key documents in regard to both poles of our paradox, should be read and re-read as a background to these short chapters. Secondly, it is profitable, I suggest, for us to try to rethink, not only the relation between Christ and his Church—an obvious priority in our discussion—but also the relation between Baptism and Holy Communion. Both of them sacraments of the death-and-life of Christ, both reproductions of the whole gospel of salvation—wherein are they distinct? Why has Baptism not been called a re-burial of Christ, on the analogy of the Eucharist being claimed as a sacrifice? Third—a point which will have to be taken up in the last chapter—what is the relation between the Eucharist, as the "focus" of obedience, to all "foci" of obedience throughout our lives—all sacraments and quasi-sacraments, all actions, in short, which are performed in Christ in obedience to God's will, and into each of which is cast the whole obedience of our lives? Are all these to be designated by terms similar to "the eucharistic sacrifice"? Martyrdom counted as Baptism: do lesser acts of obedience also partake of the nature of these great sacraments of obedience? Finally, it is vital, to my mind, that we should often reconsider the meaning of the terms sacrifice, priesthood, and intercession when they are used with reference to the relation between man and God or Christ and God. How often, let us ask ourselves, does the New Testament use a phrase like "Christ offered a sacrifice to God"? How far are terms of propitiation legitimate in this context? How, and in what circumstances, is Christ's intercession mentioned? How far is it true that God is the subject rather than the object of these actions? And how far, if at all, is it legitimate in such contexts to separate the actions of the Son from those of the Father?

II

THE FINISHED WORK OF CHRIST

EVERY section of Christian opinion unites to affirm the uniqueness and finality of the sacrifice of Christ. Yet it is well, for completeness' sake, that we should consider what the New Testament says about it. Besides, Christians who live for a time, as some of us do, chiefly within a circle of like-minded believers may too easily forget what a monstrous claim this seems to the outsider—how puzzling, how naïve perhaps. It is in a vehement form the "scandal of particularity"—this claim that an obscure man, put to death like two other condemned men at the same execution, and like, alas, millions of poor wretches at one time or another, achieved by his death something of such potency that its effects stretch infinitely far (if one may put it so) both backwards and forwards—backwards so as to take all past history into its embrace, forwards to the length of the human race that is to be. How can one individual conceivably be placed in such a position? Living in an unimportant corner of the Roman empire, under a second-rate provincial governor, virtually ignored by secular historians of the next and many generations—how can this person be claimed to occupy the very centre of history and of whatever lies outside and beyond history? That is the question asked hopelessly and incredulously by many earnest people who sincerely admire Jesus as a good man and a great man and a martyr.

Yet this is what all Christians from the very earliest days have persistently affirmed, in many different ways and from a variety of angles, but always with the same

conclusion. Let us not allow the unanimity of this conviction to blind us to its extraordinariness.

My purpose is now to remind you of some of the variety
exhibited by the New Testament writers in their presenta-
tion of this conviction, and of the correspondingly impressive unity of their central agreement as to the uniqueness and finality of what God in Christ has done. I said
that the Christian claim was that Jesus achieved by his
death something of such potency as to embrace the whole
of history, past and future. But the stress on the death in
that very phrase "achieved by his death" ought to remind
us of some shades of difference in the way that achievement is described. For sometimes the spotlight is indeed
sharply focused on the death itself. Here for instance are
passages in which the Cross is the focus of redemption:
"We proclaim Christ crucified, to the Jews a cause for
stumbling, and to the Greeks folly, but to those who are
summoned, whether Jews or Greeks, Christ the power of
God and the wisdom of God" (I Cor. 1^{23}); " . . . . but
now he has reconciled you in his physical body through
his death" (Col. 1^{22}, cf. Eph. 2^{16}); ". . . who himself
carried away our sins in his body to the cross" (I Pet. 2^{24}).
Sometimes, on the other hand, the stress is on the resurrection: "If Christ has not been raised, your faith is futile:
you are still in your sins" (I Cor. 15^{17}); "All praise to
the God and Father of our Lord Jesus Christ, who of his
great mercy has begotten us anew into a living hope
through the resurrection of Jesus Christ from among the
dead!" (I Pet. 1^{3}). In fact, however, taking the larger
context into account, salvation is seen as really the two
together in an inseparable unity.* "The New Testament as
a whole", wrote Gore (*The Body of Christ*, p. 258), "refuses
to allow us to separate the death from the life to which it

---

* Rom. 4^{25} (cf. 8^{10}) is possibly a distinguishing of the two, but more
probably the combination of them.   See also I Pet. 3^{18}, $^{21f.}$

leads up". But it remains true that these varieties of approach or emphasis do exist. Sometimes, again, it is the whole incarnation rather than its culmination in the death and resurrection which is viewed as the decisive act. And again, when the death in particular is considered, it is sometimes in ritual terms as the perfect cleansing sacrifice; at other times rather as the great outgoing act of personal generosity, as of a Father giving himself to reconcile his children. Readers will have already recognised in these latter allusions various types of writing within the New Testament—the Epistle to the Hebrews, of which Professor Alexander Nairne said that it met the need of those who feel the stain rather than the chain of sin, the Pauline Epistles ("God was in Christ reconciling the world unto himself"), the Johannine writings ("In him was life . . .").

Take first the primarily sacerdotal, sacrificial approach. The Synoptic Gospels, of course, give us the two great sacrificial sayings of Jesus—"his life a ransom for many" and the words of institution; but in this matter of the finality of that sacrifice, they have a further startling thing to say. They say that at the expiring cry of Jesus the veil of the Temple was torn in two:* that is to say, something terrific, something decisive happened to the centre of worship in Judaism. I find it difficult to believe that any of the Evangelists thought that that literally happened. Friends of mine with whom I have discussed this are prepared to believe that St. Mark did take it to be a literal fact. If so, I can only think that this Mark was remote from the ways of Judaism. Can you conceive of so shattering an event passing without stir or comment? But whether or not the Evangelists believed that it happened literally, at all events what they describe was a symbol of something

---

* I say "at the expiring cry" following Mk. and Mt.; Lk. places the last word from the Cross after the rending of the veil.

dramatically new and revolutionary in the relations between God and man: a quite new way of approach—an open access to God. Sacerdotally speaking, approach to God had hitherto been by specially prescribed means— the manipulation by the accredited priests of the blood of animal victims. Now (for this seems to be what the symbol of the rent veil is saying)* the way into the inner sanctum stands open; and that, because a Jew named Jesus from the Galilean town of Nazareth had died on a cross outside Jerusalem on a spring day in about 30 A.D.

So far these Gospels. The writer to the Hebrews, intensely concerned with the finality of the work of God in Christ and with its contrast with the incompleteness of the Levitical system, seized hold of that tradition about the rending of the veil, and wrought it in his poetical way into a highly charged, allusive symbol. The way into the sanctuary, he says, was not yet opened (9^8) during the previous era. But now, "brethren, . . . we have confidence to enter the sanctuary by the blood of Jesus, by the new and living way which he opened for us through the curtain, that is, through his flesh" ($10^{19f.}$, R.S.V.) I know that Westcott maintained that we should translate "a new and living way through the veil—that is the way of his flesh", dissociating the veil from his flesh. But, although one differs from Westcott at one's peril, this does seem to be one of the points at which the weight of New Testament scholarship has tended against him. The veil, the curtain, the writer seems to be saying, was in a manner of speaking Christ's own body. In one sense, indeed, the incarnation is the bridge between heaven and earth. But it is not until Christ's body is pierced and torn upon the Cross that

* There were other interpretations: the Temple rending its garments, or the egress of God from the Temple, etc. But access seems by far the most likely. It would be interesting to know how soon the transition was made from this phrase to the Te Deum's image "Thou didst open the kingdom of heaven".

the curtain is ripped down and a new way opened into God's presence—access via that human Person who was put to death.

And this tremendous fact—the final abolition of the barrier—corresponds with the complete supersession of all the apparatus of approach that went with it. (In passing we may remind ourselves that this supersession is viewed in Eph. 2[14ff.] as having led to the abolition of that other barrier, the wall of legal observance* which separated Jew from Gentile.) Once access is open to God without the limited apparatus of approach, the way is equally open for the Gentile believer. But to return to the writer to the Hebrews, the animal victims of the Levitical system, he says, could at best never be more than a repeated reminder of our need, a symbol of man's conviction that, guilty, he needed some remedy for his guilt:

> "For since the law has but a shadow of the good things to come instead of the true form of these realities, it can never, by the same sacrifices which are continually offered year after year, make perfect those who draw near. Otherwise, would they not have ceased to be offered? If the worshipers had once been cleansed, they would no longer have any consciousness of sin. But in these sacrifices there is a reminder of sin year after year. For it is impossible that the blood of bulls and goats should take away sins" (10[1-4], R.S.V.).

The very fact that sacrifices were constantly repeated bore witness to their inability to be finally efficacious: the repetition of sacrifice is its own indictment. And it is in contrast to this that the writer describes Christ's sacrifice. The animal victims were ineffective gestures. The very essence of Christ's self-offering is that it is once and for all. If it had not been effective absolutely it would have

---

* Whether or not the phrase is an allusion to the wall across the temple court. See the discussion in Masson's Commentary (Delachaux et Niestlé, 1953).

had to be repeated. But it is in fact final. As soon as he comes who instead of offering an animal victim offers himself, body and will, forthwith a new era opens and the old is outmoded:

> "Consequently, when Christ came into the world, he said,
> 'Sacrifices and offerings thou hast not desired,
> but a body hast thou prepared for me;   [pleasure.
> in burnt offerings and sin-offerings hast thou taken no
> Then I said, 'Lo, I have come to do thy will, O God',
> as it is written of me in the roll of the book.'

When he said above, 'Thou hast neither desired nor taken pleasure in sacrifices and offerings and burnt offerings and sin-offerings' (these are offered according to the law), then he added, 'Lo, I have come to do thy will'. He abolishes the first in order to establish the second. And by that will we have been consecrated through the offering of the body of Jesus Christ once for all. And every priest stands daily at his service, offering repeatedly the same sacrifices, which can never take away sins. But when Christ had offered for all time a single sacrifice for sins, he sat down at the right hand of God, then to wait until his enemies should be made a stool for his feet. For by a single offering he has perfected for all time those who are consecrated. And the Holy Spirit also bears witness to us; for after saying,

> 'This is the covenant that I will make with them
> after those days, says the Lord:
> I will put my laws on their hearts,
> and write them on their minds,'

then he adds,

> 'I will remember their sins and their misdeeds no more.'

Where there is forgiveness of these, there is no longer any offering for sin." (10[5-18]) (R.S.V.)

The same kind of language is also used by I Peter. I Pet. 2[21ff], admittedly, uses the language of Isa. 53 which is not so clearly sacrificial in the Levitical sense. Ἀνήνεγκεν means "removed", I think, rather than "sustained" (still less, "offered"). Indeed I doubt if the idea of redemption by sheer "sustaining" is anywhere to be found in the New Testament. But I Pet. $1^{2, 19}$, 3^{18-20} are in the same sacerdotal cast and there is the same affirmation of finality with an implied contrast to the repetitive nature of the Levitical offerings: it is ἅπαξ, once for all. But as soon as one begins to enquire upon what grounds the efficacy of Christ's sacrifice is recognised as final, immediately, I think, one begins to move out from the sacerdotal analogies into something bigger still. It is not enough to say merely that the sacrifice of Jesus was perfect, for in sacrificial terminology "perfect" simply means conforming precisely to the Levitical requirements, and that a perfect sheep or bullock might do. No: the moment one gets off mere analogy and asks a basic Why? one is transported into the great realm of the dealings of a personal God with his children. The answer to the question why Christ's sacrifice is effective in contrast to the Levitical victims is twofold. First, that it is the offering not of a reluctant beast but of a voluntarily surrendered human personality. That is very clearly expressed in the passage we have just read in Heb. 10: it is an offering of willing obedience. But not a few noble men had already offered such a sacrifice—notably the Maccabaean martyrs, who are evidently in the writer's mind at the end of Chapter 11. The obedient self-offering of a personality was not a unique event. What is it, then, that marks out Christ's self-giving as a full, perfect and sufficient sacrifice? The answer to this second question is in Christology. Christ is a priest of an eternal order offering the eternally valid sacrifice:

"The former priests were many in number, because they were prevented by death from continuing in office; but he holds his priesthood permanently, because he continues forever. Consequently he is able for all time to save those who draw near to God through him, since he always lives to make intercession for them. For it was fitting that we should have such a high priest, holy, blameless, unstained, separated from sinners, exalted above the heavens. He has no need, like those high priests, to offer sacrifices daily, first for his own sins and then for those of the people; he did this once for all when he offered up himself. Indeed, the law appoints men in their weakness as high priests, but the word of the oath, which came later than the law, appoints a Son who has been made perfect forever" (Heb. $7^{23-\text{end}}$, R.S.V., with paragraphing omitted).

Thus, Christ is both perfect and representative Man and also the eternal Son of God. And this act of will is therefore not only the one perfect response of Humanity to the will of God but also it is the will of God going out to man in yearning love. This writer uses the term Mediator, I think, only metaphorically: Jesus is the negotiator of a new convenant (8^6, 12^{24}; cf. 7^{22}). But he might well have used it Christologically, as it is used in I Tim. 2^5. Christ is for him both the Man and the eternal effulgence of God's glory. That is why he bridges the gap between man and God. That is why in him acceptance is complete. That is why through his torn body, surrendered in obedience to God's love for those who tore it, the way lies open for access.

Thus almost unwittingly we have been lifted off the analogical level of ritual acts on to the level of personal dealings; and Son is the term that marks the transition. We find Jesus as representative man fulfilling that destiny of obedience and harmony with God from which Adam by transgression fell. And here we are immediately in touch also with the thinking of St. Paul. Indeed there is a striking parallel between Heb. 2 and Phil. $2^{6\text{ff.}}$. In Heb. 2 the ideal for man, described in Psalm 8, is contrasted with man's present sorry state of defeat and frustration. But, says the writer, there is one in whom we see man's destiny completely realised—Jesus who because of his obedience in death has been crowned with the glory and honour due to man.* In Phil. 2 similarly we find the pre-existent one coming and wholly sharing the lot of man, obedient absolutely, even to the very limit of death itself; and accordingly realising the destiny of glory which is God's design. It is, as has often been suggested, a reversal of Adam's pride and fall. This, in contrast to the story of the Fall, is humility and exaltation—and that, on behalf of all mankind. I believe also that Phil. 2[6ff.] is virtually a Son of Man passage. Here is the eclipsed and suffering Son of Man (σχήματι εὑρεθεὶς ὡς ἄνθρωπος, "being found in human form", R.S.V.) ultimately vindicated and exalted (as in the clouds of heaven) and given the title of Lord.

But now that we are on Pauline territory, let us take one step back and then one step further forward. Stepping back, we can notice that St. Paul, no less than the writer to the Hebrews, is capable of viewing the Incarnation in terms of a new dispensation—a superseding of the old. The era of "faith" succeeds that of "law"; man "comes of age"; Christ is both the goal and the end of the old era (Gal. 3[23] —4[7]; and Rom. 10[4]). The step forward is into a kind of explanation of forgiveness in terms of the unique event. For we have looked at the finality of the death of Christ in terms of the absolute sacrifice, superseding all the victims of the Levitical law. We have seen also how Jesus, as perfect man, is man rendering obedience to God; and how, as the Son of God, he is also God working in man for reconciliation. And now we can add that he is the final explanation (so far as that word applies to such mysteries at all) of forgiveness. There was full recognition of the fact of forgiveness in the Old Testament, not only in the sacrificial system which, nominally at least, only applied for the most part to ritual sins, but in the plain straight-

* I think that it is much the most telling exegesis of this passage to take vv. 6-8 (the Psa. 8 quotation) as applying not specifically to Christ but to man as he is meant to be. The reference to Christ then comes in v. 9 with great force.

forward proclamation of pardon. David said "I have sinned against the Lord"; Nathan said "The Lord also hath put away thy sin". "The sacrifices of God", says the Psalmist, "are a broken spirit". God's free forgiveness had often been proclaimed before the Incarnation. The free graciousness of God was no new idea. But it was proclaimed unexplained, in uneasy tension with the conviction of God's righteousness. How could it be, when you came to think of it, that the holy and righteous God could forgive? That was an absolutely insoluble problem until it was seen that the holy God himself met the sin, accepted its entail, entered into its costliness, suffered redemptively in his own Son. Then at least it became clear—however mysterious and unsearchable God's ways must always remain to us—that here was no overlooking of guilt or trifling with forgiveness; no external treatment of sin, but a radical, a drastic, a passionate and absolutely final acceptance of the terrible situation, and an absorption by the very God himself of the fatal disease so as to neutralise it effectively: ". . . whom God put forward as an expiation by his blood, to be received by faith. This was to show God's righteousness, because in his divine forbearance he had passed over former sins; it was to prove at the present time that he himself is righteous and that he justifies him who has faith in Jesus" (Rom. 3[25f.], R.S.V.).

There for once St. Paul does step aside from his essentially activist, practical preaching of the fact of salvation, to say a word about its how and why. And his explanation turns on the finality and uniqueness of Christ. For a different purpose, and in quite a different context, the absolute priority of the Son over creation is linked in Colossians also with the finality of his salvation—the new creation: "He is . . . the first-born of all creation; . . . the first-born from the dead . . ." (Col. 1[15, 18], R.S.V.). He is uniquely Man—"Adam" is applicable to Christ in a new and absolute sense (I Cor. 15^{45}). The Man Christ Jesus: here is the heart of the mystery. Whatever angle you approach it from, you always reach this centre: in Jesus God is at work uniquely, with incomparable intensity. The Incarnation is something absolute and final because of its unique quality: an act of creation only comparable to God's initial creation.

The Johannine writings, in their own special idiom, tell the same story. The Word of God is manifested in some degree in all God's creation. But when the Word became flesh and dwelt among us that was the crowning, the unique event: we beheld his glory, the glory as of the only begotten of the Father—the Father's unique Son—full of grace and truth. That is the Pauline πρωτότοκος, first-born, set in an even wider context of thought. This unique Word of God, the convergence of all God's words, this life and light and love absolute, this Son who is subject to the Father and, by virtue of this subjection, one with him: he it is alone who at the crown of his achievement, reigning from the Tree, can cry the τετέλεσται, "it is finished". And although very broadly it may be true that whereas for St. Paul Christ saves by his death, for the Fourth Evangelist it is by his life, yet for the Fourth Evangelist too the death is the decisive thing. The Good Shepherd lays down his life; "I if I be lifted up . . ."; "except a grain of wheat fall into the ground and die . . ."

We need not labour the finality of Jesus of Nazareth further: it is clear enough, though many more examples might be quoted. Sometimes in a deliberately theological way, sometimes as though it were narrative—a "documentary"—the "scandal of particularity" is ruthlessly forced upon us by the New Testament wherever we turn. Even if in the most theological of the Gospels it is said that Abraham rejoiced to see Christ's day, yet it is still that Christ who is uniquely manifested under Pontius Pilate.

C

It is this Lamb alone who removes the sin of the whole world; he alone whose death is to be available for the whole world. It will be for the next chapter to enquire how, despite this anchorage in time, the saving work of God also runs continuously through history like a perennial stream of blessing.

But meanwhile, one further observation. If we speak in terms of Sacraments, it is Baptism which provides the "focus" for this once-and-for-all aspect of redemption. Both Baptism and the Holy Communion are sacraments of the death of Christ; but Baptism especially represents the finality and unrepeatability of it. For any one individual it is once and for all in his life. It is the sacrament *par excellence* of the once-and-for-allness of salvation. As Christ's incarnation, his death, burial and resurrection, are the world's Baptism (as recent writers have been reminding us)* so each person's Baptism is his point of contact with that final achievement. Hence, of course, the problem of post-Baptismal sin which may have begun to show itself in Heb. 6 and 10; though for my part I believe that, at least in Ch. 10, the Eucharist also can be detected, and that the crux is not post-Baptismal sin as such, but apostasy—changing sides from that of the Crucified to that of the crucifiers.

To that passage we shall have occasion to return later, if only for a moment and for another purpose. For the present, we break the matter off on this unresolved chord— the separateness, the finality, the stark uniqueness of the Incarnation: the centrality for all Christian thinking of the Jesus of history.

* See O. Cullmann, *Baptism in the New Testament and Les Sacrements dans l'Évangile Johannique*; and J. A. T. Robinson in *The Scottish Journal of Theology*, vol. 6, no. 3 (Sept. 1953), pp. 257ff.

III

THE WORK OF CHRIST CONTINUING

In the last chapter we were reminded of the striking unanimity of the New Testament regarding the finality and uniqueness of God's work in Jesus Christ—a unanimity the more striking because of the obvious differences of approach in the various writers, and their freedom from dogmatic regimentation. Nothing could be clearer than that the Christian Gospel refuses, as long as it is true to itself, to surrender this "scandal of particularity". Once and for all at a given time in history God visited and redeemed his people. Nothing can add to the completeness and finality of that declaration.

And yet it is more than a declaration. That is an axiom for Christians and it carries important corollaries. It is the approach of the living God—the personal approach of the living God—to man. And a personal approach to persons is by its very nature something which cannot be confined within a statement, or limited to a proposition. St. Paul may, on a rare occasion, step aside contemplatively (as we have seen) to say that the death of Christ, expiation of sins, explains how God was able to forgive: it was because he was that sort of character—one who was ready to suffer, one who deals realistically with sin, not (as it might have appeared) passing it over, but sacrificially expiating. But much more commonly St. Paul, like the other writers of the New Testament, is concerned with the practice, not the rationale, of evangelism: with the Gospel as power rather than as demonstration: not with explaining so much as with applying the Gospel. For it is the power of God leading to salvation—leading, that is, to total soundness, completeness and integrity of personality. Like the miracles of Jesus, it is more than a manifestation: it is a deed of power.

If, then, the Gospel is more than a declaration, if it is something which we do not merely know about but experience, essentially God's action to reconcile estranged man to himself, then it follows that the uniqueness and finality of his action in Jesus Christ is not the uniqueness of discontinuity, nor the finality of a dead and static thing. There can never be an end absolutely to this reconciliation, for it is the living God at work and it is part and parcel of the fellowship which issues from his work and in which it is perpetuated. And thus it was that the physical body of Christ, given up to death and raised from death, brought with it that fellowship which we call the Church, the Body of Christ. "Destroy this temple, and in three days I will raise it up again". He spake of the temple of his body. And in a sense, too, the Church was continuous with the People of God of the old dispensation. The unique incarnation, for all its uniqueness and finality, is found to be the centre of history—not discontinuous; a great flowing stream, not a separate draught of water; the apex of a pyramid, not an unattached point in mid-air. Or, better, it is the point of intersection of the two lines which, narrowing as the faithful remnant showed itself to be a minority, and converging to vanishing point when the remnant came to be one perfect Man, yet diverge again as that one Man becomes the growing point of a new society.

Final, absolute, unique; yet not static nor discontinuous. No diagram that one can invent to represent the position of Jesus in history can detach him from it. Here is a profoundly important matter for a doctrine of the Church; and it is part of the universally agreed doctrine of the Person of Christ. If in any sense the Incarnation is continuous with the People of God before it, then in some sense redemption must be continued in the Church after it. What does this mean?

As we stand on the brink of great doctrines, easily perverted into great heresies, let us with childlike simplicity recall ourselves to that most perfectly drawn of human analogies, the story of the Prodigal Son, to use it simply as a picture of the reciprocal quality of reconciliation. In trying to find my way through matters which are too difficult for me, I constantly take refuge in this human analogy. And such refuge, I think, is not a retreat from reality. On the contrary, it provides a salutary touchstone of our soundness. For after all, there are no higher, no profounder categories known to us than the personal; and the reconciliation of a son by and to a father provides surer terms than the most elaborate sub-personal analogies of ransom, bond or sacrifice, or the most abstruse abstracts of metaphysics, however valuable they are as contributory explanation. What then can we find in this homely analogy that may help us in relating God's once-and-for-all to our repetitive needs? The Father's act of running out to meet his returning penitent is datable and tangible, and to that extent complete. We could say, that is the spot in the road where they met; here they flung their arms round one another, here the tears fell. It was at such and such a time, on such and such a day. Done! Once and for all that reconciliation had taken place. The boy could see, as he looked at his father, what suffering had gone to that reconciling love, how costly it had been. But it is done; and there is joy unspeakable. What is more, it is done by the father's forthgoing initiative. The son came home, true; but the father it was who alone could initiate the offer of restoration.

Yet no reconciliation is one-sided. Because it is between persons, not automatic, not mechanical, it has to be both received and reciprocated. The son progressively responds. First the amazement—the difficulty in believing it; then the gradual acceptance, the picking up of loose threads, the recovery of lost ground: a process. And then, the sorest test of all; the resentful, censorious elder brother. His attitude is so easily intelligible, and yet so hard to accept. Psychologically we can easily understand that outraged elder brother's feelings; but how difficult the younger brother is going to find it to accept him, and make allowance for him, and forgive him. Here is the test: can the younger brother sacrificially enter into his father's conciliatory attitude? Can he align his will with his father's will for the wholeness of the family? Can he humbly accept censure, gently meet coldness with love, win and woo and accept the pain? In a sense it all depends now on him. Once and for all, the father's attitude speaks reconciliation: can the younger brother cast away his *amour-propre* into that great pool of love and self-giving, and throw in his lot with this reconciling power? The family's completion depends on that. If the parable, originally, in all likelihood, about pious and self-righteous Jews in contrast to the disreputable, came soon to be applied to Jewish Christians over against Gentiles welcomed into the Church, it became poignant indeed: can Gentiles in their new-found access to God—such as we were considering in the previous chapter—be sacrificially gentle and understanding towards their resentful elder brothers in Christ?

I need not pursue the analogy: you see the point. Acceptance of forgiveness and transmission of it—these are not merely addenda to the Father's reconciling love. However much the initiative is his, yet these, too, are a part of it. The process is a living, personal, organic one and must be a growing and expanding—a continually expanding—one. That helps us, I think, to read Col. 1[24] with understanding. St. Paul rejoices that his sufferings help to complete what is lacking of the afflictions of Christ. This seems to mean two things. First, that the Christian's sufferings (in this case the Apostle's) are a share in Christ's sufferings, because the Christian and Christ are somehow connected. To be in Christ is of course to share Christ's sufferings, and there are always more of them in the future for each of us. Secondly it means that there is a quota of sufferings which the whole Church, the corporate Christ, has to exhaust before God's plan of salvation is complete; and the Apostle rejoices to take his share—or more than his share—of these. Thus "the afflictions of Christ" are both Christ's historical sufferings, mystically shared and entered into in each Christian's sufferings, and the corporate Christ's, the Christian Church's afflictions. The two are in that sense one. There is plenty of evidence that the Christians took over the Jewish apocalyptic idea of the Messianic woes; and there was a certain quota of these to be completed before the end could come. So the afflictions of the (corporate) Christ, the Messianic community, were a necessary prelude to the consummation, and their endurance was cause for rejoicing. But also there is this more mystical conception of sharing Christ's Cross. A. R. George, in his admirable book *Communion with God* (p. 184) says: "Paul does not mean merely that the Christian experiences the sufferings of Christ after Him in thought, imagination, or sympathy, nor merely that his own actual sufferings are endured with Christ or for the sake of Christ (though all these ideas are present), but that *his own actual sufferings are a real participation in Christ's sufferings, suffered by virtue of his communion with Christ*" (my italics).

In any case, the Church has more to suffer. The corporate Christ's afflictions have yet to be completed. But in no case does the incompleteness lie in the divine power or source of redemption—only in the accepting, entering into, implementing, and transmitting of it. The Prodigal Son is called upon to respond; the family has to enter into the realisation of the reparation. This seems to be the sense—a carefully safeguarded and qualified sense—in which Christ's sacrifice can be spoken of as constantly renewed. And we are bound to add that the sufferings of those who lived before Christ must also be gathered up and reckoned in the process. If the Church's sufferings are in this sense a sharing of Christ's sacrifice, so are Israel's sufferings an anticipation of it. If the Eucharist is in any sense a sacrifice related to Calvary, so was the obedience of Abraham. Since Christ is the centre of history and, though a real individual, is yet more than an individual, he gathers up into himself all the god-ward activities of all his people and creatures, past, present and future: he is one with mankind and with creation.

We have now returned from the consideration of the reciprocal nature of redemption to the question of Christ and the Trinity. I often revert in this connection to Helen Waddell's story of *Peter Abelard*.* Abelard and Thibault hear a sudden cry. It is a poor little rabbit in a trap, and when they reach it, they are just too late.

It lay for a moment breathing quickly, then in some blind recognition of the kindness that had met it at the last, the small head thrust and nestled against his arm, and it died.

It was that last confiding thrust that broke Abelard's heart. He looked down at the little draggled body, his mouth shaking. "Thibault," he said, "do you think there is a God at all? Whatever has come to me, I earned it. But what did this one do?"

Thibault nodded.

"I know," he said. "Only—I think God is in it too."

Abelard looked up sharply.

* Constable, 1933, pp. 289ff.

"In it? Do you mean that it makes Him suffer, the way it does us?"

Again Thibault nodded.

"Then why doesn't He stop it?"

"I don't know," said Thibault. "Unless—unless it's like the Prodigal Son. I suppose the father could have kept him at home against his will. But what would have been the use? All this," he stroked the limp body, "is because of us. But all the time God suffers. More than we do."

Abelard looked at him, perplexed.

"Thibault, when did you think of all this?"

Thibault's face stiffened. "It was that night," he said, his voice strangled. "The things we did to—to poor Guibert. He—" Thibault stopped. "I could not sleep for nights and nights. And then I saw that God suffered too. And I thought I would like to be a priest."

"Thibault, do you mean Calvary?"

Thibault shook his head. "That was only a piece of it— the piece that we saw—in time. Like that." He pointed to a fallen tree beside them, sawn through the middle. "That dark ring there, it goes up and down the whole length of the tree. But you only see it where it is cut across. That is what Christ's life was; the bit of God that we saw. And we think God is like that, because Christ was like that, kind, and forgiving sins and healing people. We think God is like that for ever, because it happened once, with Christ. But not the pain. Not the agony at the last. We think that stopped."

Abelard looked at him, the blunt nose and the wide mouth, the honest troubled eyes. He could have knelt before him.

"Then, Thibault," he said slowly, "you think that all this," he looked down at the little quiet body in his arms, "all the pain of the world, was Christ's cross?"

"God's cross," said Thibault. "And it goes on."

"The Patripassian heresy," muttered Abelard mechanically. "But, oh God, if it were true. Thibault, it must be. At least, there is something at the back of it that is true. And if we could find it—it would bring back the whole world."

No doubt there *is* heresy there if it is stated without counterbalance; but there is more than "something at the back of it that is true". Here we have been driven again to

face one of the most arresting and important of all Christo-
logical terms, the inclusive Christ as the Second Adam,
the New Man, the beginning of God's new creation. That
Jesus was a man, not merely mankind, has been strenuously
and rightly re-affirmed by the late Dr. D. Baillie: he
protested against the depersonalisation of calling Christ
"Man" instead of "a man"—"Humanity" rather than an
individual, Jesus of Nazareth.* That I am sure is right. But
the fact remains that if to call Christ Humanity is to call
him by too abstract a term, to limit him to an individual
is equally to fail to do justice to the facts. For his individ-
uality is somehow inclusive: he is representative Man; he
includes mankind and in fact fulfils the destiny of man, as
those New Testament writers saw who applied to Jesus the
ideal picture of man in Psalm 8, and who likened him to
Adam. Therefore Christ's obedience is man's obedience.
And if man, as a result, begins to obey, that may be called
Christ's obedience in man. There *is*, then, a continuity in
some sense between Christ and man, and between man's
obedience derived from Christ's, and Christ's perfect,
underived holiness.

And this real element of continuity may help to explain
the sense in which, elsewhere in the New Testament,
terms of intercession are used of the atoning work of
Christ. We must think more about this in the next chapter,
but meanwhile we recall that in Rom. 8[27, 34] the Spirit and
Christ are said to plead for us; in Heb. 7[25] the Great High
Priest lives continually to make intercession; in John 14-16
the Spirit is our Paraclete or Vindicator, and so, in I John 2[1],
is Christ again. The work of Christ—God's work of reconciliation in him—achieved once and for all, is, so to speak,
a standing intercession, for it is Man as he ought to be. Its
efficacy remains continually active, just as the father's act
of welcome to the returning Prodigal Son—a single and

* See *God was in Christ* (Faber, 1948), pp. 86f.

datable act, but one which was only the "focal" point of a long-formed character and constant activity—is a standing intercession (if you like), all the time realistically facing sin's entail, saying all the time "It was meet that we should make merry and be glad: for this my son was dead and is alive again, he was lost and is found". The father's character is the real continuum. He is that sort of father: that is why reconciliation can take place. God is a self-incarnating God: that is how man is related to him.

Thus the one, final, definitive act of God in Jesus Christ is also his continuous act. It is, in terms of Greek grammar, like the combining of an aorist tense—he saved us, ἔσωσεν —with a resultant perfect—we are saved, σεσωσμένοι—and, indeed, with a present tense of process—we are being saved, σωζόμενοι. But Christ is never, I think, actually spoken of as continuing to suffer with us (unless you count Heb. 4[15], "we have not a high priest who is unable to sympathize with our weaknesses"—and even there the past is prominent—"but one who . . . has been tempted").* Still less is he described as offering himself or being offered again, or as being crucified with us or dying with us. St. Paul is crucified with Christ; but in the only place in the New Testament where re-crucifixion of Christ is mentioned (Heb. 6[6]) it is a description of apostasy, not (as such) of the work of redemption. Yet, because we are incorporated in Christ, the work of salvation is in a sense actually continuing among us: it is not ours, but it is Christ's in us. That is what is meant perhaps by his continued intercession.

Thus the Church is not the source of salvation, but it is the transmitter of salvation and the sphere in which God's saving work continues. It is not strictly speaking the extension of the Incarnation, for incarnation by long usage

* N.B. Rom. 6[10], where the tenses are significant: he *died* once and for all; but he *lives*.

means God's fulness, πλήρωμα, in flesh; and the Church, although indwelt by God the Holy Spirit, is not all-divine as an incarnation on that showing must be, any more than the great men and prophets before Christ, though indwelt by God, were incarnations. Or else, if God be called incarnate in the prophets, then *a fortiori* the Church is the extention of the Incarnation; but then the moment we say this and use "incarnate" so, we are blurring precisely that uniqueness of Christ which was the theme of the previous chapter. We must not try to have it both ways in our use of "incarnation". Not yet does God's fulness, his πλήρωμα, reside in us as it does in Christ; the Church is not co-equal with God as Christ is; there is no absolute *communicatio idiomatum* between Christ and his Body the Church. Thus it seems to me impossible fully to iden-tify an act of obedience in a Christian (including his partici-pation in the sacrament of obedience) with the absolute and perfect act of obedience by God incarnate in Christ. Each Christian act of obedience is indeed Christ's obedience in us; but not therefore identifiable with his own one-hundred-per-cent obedience in his own person. Hence Dr. C. H. Dodd's phrase "in solidarity with him we have died and risen again" seems more faithful to the New Testament than Dr. E. F. Scott's "a repetition in the believer of Christ's death and resurrection".* It is that the believer is present at Christ's death rather than that Christ is present at his: Paul taught not so much that the believer *repeats* Christ's experience, as that he is *with Christ* in Christ's experience.

But on any showing Christ is closely concerned in the activity of his Church: the Church's sufferings are his. And the Church, if not fully an incarnation, is destined to

* See E. Best, *One Body in Christ* (S.P.C.K., 1955), p. 46 (quoting from the Moffatt Commentaries on *Romans*, by Dodd, and *Colossians*, by Scott).

grow up in all things into Christ's full stature, and who can say what may not some day be? Is it possible (one shrinks from so daring a speculation) that the Church of today may be to the Church of the End—the coming Great Church—what the prophets of Israel were to Christ? Is it that one day God will become incarnate again, but this time not as a perfect individual, Jesus of Nazareth, but as his Holy Spirit incarnate in the perfect society, the Bride? Is that the Day of the Lord?

IV

THE EUCHARISTIC SACRIFICE

IN the two preceding chapters I have tried to formulate successively, first the Christian conviction of the absolute uniqueness and finality of what God incarnate in Christ had done, and second the equally strong conviction that in a sense that final and completed act is yet being implemented in the life of the Church which is the Body of Christ. The body of his flesh is so related to his Body the Church that the Church's afflictions are the implementing of his passion under Pontius Pilate. And indeed the afflictions of the Old Testament people of God—and of the true and upright everywhere—must in some way be woven into the texture of that Passion. Though unique, it is not altogether discontinuous, just as Christ himself, while unique, was not discontinuous with the Law and the Prophets before him. God incarnate in the form of an individual man is somehow related to God dwelling corporately within a society, though an *incarnation* (using that word in the stricter, narrower sense) of this corporate sort has never yet been seen. Perhaps it is yet to come.

Baptism, as I said, is the sacrament *par excellence* of the once-and-for-all finality: it stands for the finished work of Christ as it is applied to each individual's life. Holy Communion, so far as it may be contrasted with Baptism, is different in precisely this respect that it essentially represents repetition. Within any given individual's life, there can be no repetition of Baptism. Where there is sacramental repetition of the Gospel, it is in the Eucharist. Thus, of the two, the Eucharist is the more particularly connected with our second theme—the implementing, the repetition, the continuation. And, the mode of this continuation being a theologically difficult matter, it is hardly surprising if Holy Communion has, alas, become the battleground on which many a champion of one insight or another has fought desperately against the opposite. That, no doubt, is partly due, not only to sheer sin and selfishness, but also to our inevitable human limitations which make it almost impossible to get one part of the truth sharply into focus without finding that the remainder looks blurred and repellent and arouses our antagonism.

"Ever since the sixteenth century," wrote the late Dom Gregory Dix (*The Shape of the Liturgy*, pp. 613f.), "we Anglicans have been so divided over eucharistic doctrine, and we are today so conscious of our divisions, that there is scarcely any statement that could be made about either the eucharist or our own rite which would not seem to some of one's fellow churchmen to call for immediate contradiction on conscientious grounds. It is quite understandable. These things go deep behind us. Two archbishops of Canterbury have lost their lives and a third his see, in these quarrels. One king has been beheaded and another dethroned; many lesser men have suffered all manner of penalties from martyrdom downwards on one side and another. These things have left their traces, tangling and confusing our own approach to the matter in all sorts of irrelevant ways. Besides the conscious inheritance of different intellectual and doctrinal positions from the past, and inextricably mingled with it, is another inherited world of unconscious misunderstandings, prejudices, assumptions, suspicions, which are only accidentally bound up with theological terms and which yet come into play instantly and secretly and quite irrationally with their use. To spring the word 'transubstantiation' on the company without preparation in certain circles (or the names 'Tyburn' or 'Barnes' in others) is to invite a reaction which springs much more from emotion than from reason."

So we need not, perhaps we must not, agonise over much

about the sin of dissension on such holy ground, sinful though it is. And at least we can give whole-hearted thanks for the privileges of the present generation, in which the Spirit of God is putting into our hands instruments for mutual understanding such as our fathers never possessed. In view of this, I hope you will agree that we can profitably consider so controversial a matter as the meaning of the eucharistic Sacrifice without violating the devotional attitude appropriate to it: indeed, pray God, it will be for the deepening of our devotion.

I venture to ask, then, at the outset: do we sacrifice at all in Holy Communion? Is this a sacrifice we are performing? I have tried in my own thinking to reckon with Dr. E. L. Mascall, and through him with De la Taille and Vonier. But I am not attempting now to argue the matter scholastically. All I am going to try to do is to explain my convictions and why I hold them, as a contribution simply to mutual understanding. This is just an individual thinking aloud, for what it is worth, in the company (as he hopes) of friends, even if at points they will think differently. You will remember the comments I cited in the first chapter. One of them urged the importance of emphasising the fact that at Eucharist the Church offers the whole of the material world to be dedicated to the service of God—all that the offertory procession expresses. Another stressed the aspect of pleading—pleading before God the efficacy of Christ's sacrifice. A third wished to wipe out all idea of sacrifice, except in the sense that the worshippers, receiving the benefits of Christ's once-and-for-all sacrifice, then offer themselves in devotion as response. We could have multiplied voices, conflicting, complementary, modifying, at endless length. What then are we to say? What do we do at Holy Communion?

Let me in part anticipate my own conclusions, and then discuss them a little.

We do offer sacrifice at Holy Communion. Starting from the less controversial, at least we offer (as the Prayer of Oblation explicitly says) the sacrifice of ourselves, our souls and bodies, of our praise and thanksgiving. The whole Church offers up her praise and her obedience to God; and with it (in the vein of Romans 8 and of all that is implied in the Christian doctrine of man) is offered the whole creation of which man is the representative: "Man the High Priest of Nature". The New Testament certainly uses terms of sacrifice for this offering of praise and obedience: Rom. 12[1], Heb. 13[15f.], I Pet. 2[5], are examples, and the Prayer of Oblation deliberately echoes such language.

But can we say more? Do we hereby offer up not only ourselves, but Christ's obedience, or rather does he through us offer up his own obedience? Well, any obedience which we can offer is imperfect, derived, secondary—a result only of Christ's perfect obedience; but, with these limitations and to that extent, it is Christ's obedience in us: in that sense, our sacrifice is Christ's sacrifice in us. *In that sense* who could deny that the Eucharist was Christ offering himself?

Yet, to my mind the New Testament's usage which we considered in the last chapter—as a rule distinguishing between what Christ did and what Christians do, reluctant to speak of Christ doing these things in us, far more ready to speak of our doing them in Christ, of our participating in Christ's sacrifice, and death, and life—is a pointer to the importance of maintaining the perspective in which the uniqueness and special nature of Christ's perfect offering is clearly visible. I would therefore sooner speak of the Eucharist as a uniting of our offering with Christ's, and that in virtue, and as a result, of our first receiving from him the gift which he alone can offer.

But before we can get any further, it seems to me that one misconception must at this point be faced and cleared

D

away. Priestly terms have frequently been used in our discussion—necessarily, since we are discussing New Testament doctrine, and terms of priesthood, sacrifice and intercession occur in the New Testament. But in what sense are these words to be understood? Not—let us be clear at the outset—in a propitiatory sense. The sacrifice of Christ was not, according to the New Testament, propitiatory—still less, then, is there anything propitiatory about any derived or related sacrifice of the Church. It is a grave misfortune that the misleading word "propitiation" has got into the English scriptures at Rom. 3^{25} and I John 2^2, and so into the Prayer Book. It has been to my mind conclusively shown that the remarkable thing about the words ἱλαστήριος and ἱλασμός, used in those verses, is precisely that, whereas their secular use was indeed of propitiating an alienated deity or person, in the Bible generally, and certainly in the New Testament, the amazing revelation of God's redemptive dealings with man has spun the word round face-about, and has compelled it to have, as its object, not God but sin. It is not that Christ or man tries to propitiate God, but that God in Christ expiates sin: God—marvel of marvels—suffering in order to neutralise man's sin. The very initiative is God's: how then can God be said to be propitiated? He is the subject of the verb, no longer its object.

In the New Testament, then, the idea of a propitiating of God on any showing never comes into view. Terms of intercession or pleading are, it is true, associated with Jesus as though he had to plead man's cause before an alienated Judge. But can we possibly press even this figure in such a way as to allow that conclusion? In Romans 8^{34} it does not look like it. In Hebrews it is of course bound up with the whole analogy of the Day of Atonement ritual, and, as we shall see, it is Christ's vindicated humanity which pleads. Thus it must be a vivid way of saying that what God incarnate has done is so realistic a dealing with sin that his morality is inviolate when he forgives us, when he clears the guilty. So in I John 2². We simply cannot allow these juridical terms—part of the apparatus of "theodicy"—to drive a wedge between the Persons of the Trinity. If we use the figure, it must be held firmly as an internal dialogue—God's own self-sacrifice meeting his justice. "The modern conception", wrote Wescott in his great Commentary on Hebrews (p. 230) "of Christ pleading in heaven His Passion, 'offering His blood' on behalf of men has no foundation in the Epistle. His glorified humanity is the eternal pledge of the absolute efficacy of His accomplished work. He pleads, as older writers truly expressed the thought, by His Presence on the Father's Throne".

I must add here that for myself I remain wholly unconvinced by the attempts to make the *anamnesis* ("this do in *remembrance* of me") mean that God is here reminded of what Christ has wrought: "Do this to remind God of me".* Reminding God of man's deserts is indeed a conception not absent from the Old Testament; but I cannot find room for it (or for the adapted form—reminding God of Christ's merits) in the New Testament. Nor do I think the linguistic arguments for doing so are at all persuasive.†

And all this is what makes me a little uncomfortable even with that familiar verse of Bright's extremely beautiful hymn quoted, as we saw in Chapter I, by Mr. Walls:

> We here present, we here spread forth to thee
> That only offering perfect in thine eyes.

Of course it can be justified in terms of that internal dialogue within the Godhead—God's mercy pleading with

---

* See the discussion in J. Jeremias, *The Eucharistic Words of Jesus* (English translation by A. Ehrhardt, Blackwell, 1955), pp. 162ff.

† See D. Jones in J.T.S. (new series) vi. Part 2 (October 1955). pp. 183ff.

his justice. It can be justified in terms of Christ's obedience being inherent in every act of man's obedience. But both because of my hesitation in identifying those two obediences, and because of my fear of propitiatory language, I feel a reluctance about such phrases.

At any rate, you will, I am sure, agree with me that it is vital to remove from our minds any crudely propitiatory conception of the sacrifice of Christ. Yet in the same breath we must now add that the realistic dealing with sin which I suppose it is the chief purpose of that language of propitiation, mistakenly so translated, and that language of vindication, to safeguard, is intensely important and as vividly present in the Eucharist as can be. Christ's glorified humanity, representing the costly obedience of mankind— God's own costly obedience to his own laws, incarnate in mankind—is of absolute efficacy. Nothing could be clearer than that the Gospel, focused in the Lord's Supper, is a Gospel of God's final and effective and infinitely sacrificial and costly dealing with sin: a Gospel of obedience to the will of God achieved within man, sin's entail met in man by maintaining perfect obedience in the face of the worst that man's sin could do.

But this obedient humanity? Is not this the point at which we return to the question of our offering at the Eucharist? It is true, admittedly, that never except in Jesus Christ has mankind assumed its proper attitude of obedience to the Father; and that it is through this obedience of the perfect Man alone that sinful humanity can approach the Father. Or, putting it in unitarian terms, it is through the divine Father's initiative alone that we, the prodigal sons, can come back into our Father's home, and through no merit of our own. Yet, as we have been at pains to see, some active response is necessary. Unless the father's initiative and gracious forgiveness so move the son that he responds with all the obedience at his command

—whole-heartedly so far as his heart is his to give—he cannot in the nature of the case come in; or at any rate he cannot stay inside the home. Unless his obedience is laid on the altar with the father's sacrificial love, there is small hope of the elder brother being won. In short, it is in fellowship with the father—in a union of will with him— that the son (still speaking in terms of the parable, not in Trinitarian terms of the Persons of the Godhead) can be his true self and make his contribution to the wholeness of the family. And it is in communion with God in Jesus Christ that we are caught up into his work. The key to any understanding that may be given us of what happens when man is born into God's activity in Jesus Christ is this κοινωνία "fellowship", this being ἐν Χριστῷ, "in Christ". Our own obedience is at best a derived, imperfect obedience. But in union with Christ's perfect obedience it is offered to God; and may it not be said that every imperfect offering of our obedience is both derived from, and again joined in the stream of Christ's obedient love which flows continually to the Father? For it is a stream of continuous flowing; and one of our difficulties is precisely that, in rightly affirming the unique and once-and-for-all nature of Christ's offering, we yet have to find some way of doing justice to its continued movement: the tree-trunk is sawn through only at one particular point; yet the marks which it there reveals in fact run continuously throughout its length. It is this dilemma, the dilemma of man as the Great Amphibian, living in history, yet aware of the beyond, which Dom Gregory Dix so clearly illuminated in *The Shape of the Liturgy*, when he showed that, when once the redemptive action was limited to the Cross, then the Eucharist had to be conceived of either as in some way a repetition or iteration of the redeeming act of Christ, or else, with the Reformers (who stressed the finality of the Cross), as only a remembering of the past:

". . . the practical confining of the redeeming action of Christ (into which the eucharist enters) to Calvary", he wrote, "led to serious and unnecessary difficulties. Being wholly within history and time, the passion is wholly in the *past*—the only moment of redemption which is so wholly confined to the past. The church at the eucharist can only be conceived to enter into a wholly past action in one of two ways, either purely *mentally* by remembering or imagining it; or else, if the entering into it is to have any objective reality outside the mind, by way of some sort of *repetition* or iteration of the redeeming act of Christ. Thus the way was not so much laid open as forced upon the church to that general late mediaeval notion of some *fresh* sacrifice of Christ, and His immolation again at every eucharist. There was no other way by which the reality of the eucharistic action could be preserved on the mediaeval understanding of it; yet the unbroken tradition of liturgy and theology alike insisted on this reality. And since the eucharistic action was now viewed as the act of the priest alone—though the liturgy itself continued to state a different view ('We Thy servants together with Thy holy people offer unto Thee . . .'), there was no escaping the idea that the priest sacrifices Christ afresh at every mass. However hard they tried to conciliate this view of the matter with the doctrine of the Epistle to the Hebrews of the one oblation for sins, perfect and complete (so far as history and time are concerned) on Calvary, the mediaeval theologians, and the party of the old religion at the English Reformation, never quite got away from the necessity of defending the reality of the eucharistic sacrifice as in some sense an iteration of the sacrifice of Christ at the hands of the priest, even though they insisted that it was not a *new* sacrifice.

"The Reformers, on the other hand, likewise carrying on the mediaeval insistence on the passion as the whole redeeming act into which the eucharist enters, took the other alternative. Since the passion is wholly in the past, the church now can only enter into it purely mentally, by *remembering* and imagining it. There is for them, therefore, no real sacrifice whatever in the eucharist. The external rite is at the most an acted memorial, *reminding* us of something no longer present. . . .

"All that constitutes the eucharistic action on this view is the individual's reception of the bread and wine. But this is only a 'token'. The real eucharistic action (if 'action' is not a misleading term) takes place mentally, in the isolated secrecy of the individual's mind. The eucharistic action is thereby altogether deprived of its old corporate significance; it is practically abolished even as a corporate act. The external action must be done by each man for himself; the real eucharistic action goes on separately, even if simultaneously, within each man's mind. . . .

"Even the external rite is no longer a *corporate* rite integral to the performance of the real eucharistic action, but a common preparation for it, designed only to prepare each communicant subjectively to perform it for himself. . . . There is no possibility of pleading the eucharist for one another, or for the dead in Christ; though we may pray together *at* it (not *by* it) as we intercede at other times. . . .

"All this is a strictly logical and inevitable development from the protestant basis, and the proof of this is that it was the development everywhere followed by later protest-antism, in spite of the hesitations of the Reformers. They would gladly have saved more of the primitive and med-iaeval devotional estimation of the eucharist, if they could. But I ask attention for the fact that it is the logical development along one line of something which in itself is Latin and mediaeval, the practical restriction of the significance of the eucharist to the passion, as the historical element in the redeeming act, seen apart from its supra-historical elements in the resurrection, ascension and eternal priesthood. Given that restriction, there is no way of entering into Christ's action but by a repetition of it however guarded, or by a mere mental remembering of it, however vivid and devout. Fifteenth-century catholicism, in effect, took the one line; protestantism, to safeguard the sovereign efficacy of the sacrifice of Christ, took the other. As regards the eucharist they are not complementary in their ideas, but strictly alternative developments of the same idea. The one can never comprehend the other" (pp. 623-625).

I should wish, greatly daring, to challenge Dix's virtual identification of the inward and the mental with that which is individual (as though the external were the only corporate). But for the moment let that pass. It is his clearly drawn dilemma that we are concerned with. Once limit redemption to Calvary, and you must either *repeat* or else only *remember*. There is, I think, a resolution of this dilemma only when we give full value to "the mystical union that is betwixt Christ and His Church" as a union of fellowship, distinguishing it at the same time from a union of identity. By κοινωνία, by being ἐν Χριστῷ, we in some way enter into his obedience; and accordingly, every offering of our obedience is both derived from, and caught up into, his obedience. Our obedience is derived from his and dependent upon it; and in the perennial stream of his obedience it goes to God. But it is not identified with it. Wescott (*Hebrews*, p. 229) referring to the High Priestly work of Christ in threefold terms as intercession, as bringing the prayers and praises of his people to God, and as securing access to the Holy Place, writes: "These three forms of Christ's work shew under the conditions of human experience what He does for humanity eternally. Our fellowship with God will grow closer, more perfect, more conscious, but still our approach to God, our worship, our spiritual harmony, must always be 'in Him' in Whom we have been incorporated."

Thus whenever we approach God it can only be in Christ or in the Spirit. Every virtue we possess and every victory won, and every thought of holiness, are his alone. But every act of derived obedience on our part, though not identical with it, is yet really joined with Christ's own obedience. And in a sacrament which is a focal point of obedience the two obediences—Christ's and ours, Christ's in ours and ours in Christ's—are offered to God together. The New Testament "with-" and "fellowship" words, the σύν-and κοινων-and ἐν Χριστῷ, are not phrases of identification-mysticism but of fellowship-mysticism. God forbid that we should countenance what Gore calls a view of which it is exceedingly difficult to bear the statement:

a view "which involves in each mass in some real sense a re-sacrificing of Christ" (*The Body of Christ*, p. 179, cf. Dix as just quoted). Incidentally if we did assert this of the Mass, would not consistency demand that we proclaimed every baptism a re-burial of Christ? A baptism is a real sharing of Christ's death and burial, and thus equally liable to be called a re-enactment of it. In each baptism, at least as really as in the Easter sepulchre, Christ is buried and rises again. But this is clearly, in the case of Baptism, in a derived, limited and specialised sense. How then can the so-called re-enactment of the death of Christ in the Eucharist be otherwise understood? As we saw in the last chapter, the present tenses in the New Testament are mostly of verbs applied to the Church, not to Christ: it is the Church with Christ, rather than Christ with the Church. We cannot speak, then, of re-sacrificing. The only New Testament passage which speaks of re-crucifying Christ relates to apostasy (Heb. 6[6]). St. Paul is crucified with Christ; he does not speak of crucifying Christ. He and his fellow-Christians are offered as a sacrifice; he does not speak of offering Christ, or even of Christ continually offering Himself.

Yet the sacrifice of Christ, complete and perfect, is nevertheless the historical focus of a continual obedience: the obedience of Christ which must be in all suffering accepted in his name and in all praise and worship and self-dedication whatever. And since this is derived from, focused, and caught up in Christ's sacrifice, it is possible (though only with careful safeguards) to speak *in that sense* of such offerings as a constant reproduction of it—a part of it, and not merely a remembering of it. In Rev. 7[14] there is mention of those who have washed their robes and made them white in the blood of the Lamb. This, of course, is applicable to all Christians as such: we all owe our cleansing to that blood. But if, as is sometimes held, this passage refers specially to martyrs, then I suggest— though this is only a guess—that it is possible that we are confronted with a striking example of the way in which Christ's once-and-for-all sacrifice might be, in certain circumstances, spoken of as repeated in each act of human obedience joined with his. The martyrs' own blood, shed in faithfulness to the Lord, turns out to be the blood of the Lamb. When their blood flowed, behold it was the blood of the Lamb. Their sacrifice was united with his—not as though theirs were independently redemptive or added anything to his, but in the sense that, being united, believer and Lord are, in that sense, one: his blood their blood, their blood his. The blood which is the sacrament of obedience is the Lord's blood: the wine which is the sacrament of obedience is, *in that sense*, the Lord's blood.

The dangers that need most strenuously to be guarded against (to repeat this once more), are, as it seems to me, the dangers of allowing any trace of a doctrine either of human merit or of propitiatory sacrifice to creep in. Christ's sacrifice is not propitiatory, but it is God's absolutely effective and final meeting of sin. Man's sacrifice is neither propitiatory nor in its own right effective or final. The Church is not identical with Christ, and its sacrifice is simply derived, as all that we have is derived, from Christ. But being thus derived, and being united with Christ's, it becomes *in this sense* a continuation of what Christ has wrought. It is (although, as we have seen, the New Testament is very chary of such expressions, and they need to be carefully qualified) Christ in us, Christ within humanity, Christ expressing man's obedience to God's loving purposes, Christ's once-and-for-all sacrifice being implemented in us. And every Eucharist is a "focal" point of that; not a mere recalling to the mind, nor yet a re-enactment; but an entering into what Christ has done —just as indeed is every symbol of obedience. For this too must be faced. It is theologically false, I am convinced, to segregate the Gospel sacraments and the ecclesiastical sacraments in any essential way (apart from degrees of authoritative institution) from all those quasi-sacramental "focal" points of obedience in life—the tangible, datable implementations of our will to serve God. The convert at the penitents' bench, the repentant person making restitution—these are using sacramental acts as channels for their acceptance of God's gift of forgiveness. All these are tangible, datable: hand-holds in the rock face of our life's ascent in time and space, points at which we grasp the once-and-for-all achievement of God's redemption. Every time a Christian or a group of Christians does something for the Lord's sake, whether it is (positively) giving a donation of blood at a transfusion centre, or going to a house to visit someone in need, or rendering some service as a community; or whether (negatively) it is refusing some pleasure because it appears to hinder the Lord's work; and whether it is an external action or a secret transaction of the soul—at all such points the stream of the sacrifice of Calvary is still seen flowing. It is (if, guardedly, we use a dichotomy of language) the Lord's obedience in us being offered up to God. "Inasmuch as ye did it unto one of the least of these my brethren, ye did it unto me" is, surely, also capable of being extended into "Inasmuch as ye did it unto God the Father, ye did it as adopted sons, united with his only Son".

William Temple (*Christus Veritas*, pp. 238f.) wrote:

> "The sacrifice of Christ is potentially but not really the sacrifice of Humanity. Our task is, by his Spirit, to take our place in that sacrifice. In the strict sense there is only one sacrifice—the obedience of the Son to the Father, and of Humanity to the Father in the Son. This was manifest in actual achievement on Calvary; it is represented in the breaking of the Bread; it is reproduced in our self-dedication

and resultant service; it is consummated in the final coming of the Kingdom."

That seems to me a marvellously comprehensive and measured statement; and for my part I would only wish to qualify or to explain, in the manner I have already tried to indicate, the word "reproduced." *Mutatis mutandis*, the same applies, from my point of view, to this, from the same context (pp. 241f.):

> "The Eucharist is a sacrifice; but we do not offer it; Christ offers it; and we, responding to His act, take our parts or shares in His one sacrifice as members of His Body. The Bread which the Church, by the hands of the priest, breaks and gives is the Body of Christ, that is, it is the Church itself.... Christ in us presents us with Himself to the Father; we in Him yield ourselves to be so presented; or to put it in other words Redeeming love so wins our hearts that we offer ourselves to be presented by the Love that redeems to the Love that created and sustains both us and all the universe."

The only phrase there which, it seems to me, goes beyond the very words of the New Testament is "Christ in us presents us with Himself to the Father"; but even that is (as I have tried to show that I recognise) implicit in the New Testament idea of Christ as the New Humanity, the Second Adam, representative Man, offering representative obedience to the Father's will. And it is to be noticed that Temple was careful to guard against a false dichotomy in his description of the Love that redeems making an offering to the Love that creates.

Thus, looking back over the themes we have pondered together, it is certain that all Christians alike agree that at Holy Communion we *declare and acknowledge* what God in Christ has done once and for all: we *declare* his finished work of redemption. We declare it, moreover, expectantly: *till he come*. We shall all agree, necessarily, that we also penitently and gratefully *receive* for ourselves this finished work: we stretch out our hands to take the proffered pledges of his love; we assimilate, by faith, the Son of God who loved us and gave himself for us. We feed upon him: we eat the Bread of Life. We agree, further, that these pledges of his love are also pledges of our *obedience*: they are our fealty, offered up to God, representing all creation dedicated to the Creator. We agree that this offering is the *result of Christ's perfect obedience*—made possible alone by him; and that it is offered *in communion with him*, in the fellowship of his sufferings: *in Christ, our offering becomes a part of his.*

Where we may differ, at least in emphasis or degree, is on the question of whether this is, therefore, *a repetition of Christ's offering*: whether *he offers himself*, or whether the present tense can only strictly be used of us *in* him. And the varying emphases here—arising, I think, from the crippling limitations of our finite minds—are of value because each stands for some great facet of the single, supremely mysterious truth.

For my own part, I feel, at present, the great importance of stressing the once-and-for-all uniqueness of Christ's sacrifice and the utterly dependent and derived character of ours. I am therefore inclined still to welcome the 1662 position of the Prayer of Oblation. Burkitt, in *Eucharist and Sacrifice** (a six penn'orth of wisdom greater than many more costly volumes) said that what he wished to change in Cranmer's plan was the rubric *Or this*, between the Prayer of Oblation and the Prayer of Thanksgiving. *And this* was Burkitt's amendment.

But most of all I am concerned to preserve the precious truth embodied in the *personal* categories of our religion (and "personal" means not "individual" only: corporate also, but personal), using the sub-personal categories only

* Heffer and Sons, 1927.

as aids and illustrations, not as controls. If we call upon God as Father, I do not see how we can find room in our worship (any more than the New Testament found room) for terms of propitiation, but rather for the infinitely greater and more marvellous Gospel of the "expiation" of sin by God himself who, in Christ, was reconciling the world unto himself—submitting to the consequences of our disobedience. And it is by entering into communion with him, by κοινωνία, in his Son Jesus Christ, that we are united with that reconciling act by the response of sons. "Communion" or "fellowship" (κοινωνία), "together with" (σύν-), and "in Christ" (ἐν Χριστῷ)—these, as I see it, are the keys to the meaning of the Eucharistic sacrifice; and they express a union not of identity but of fellowship. Organic terms are precious and illuminating; but, as Dr. Dillistone reminds us,* they are complementary to the terms of Covenant and Communion.

We have only scratched the surface of a fathomless mystery. Even to do that much is to realise its awfulness and wonder and supreme complexity. God enlighten us, and lead us forward together by his mercy into the mystery of his love as Creator, Redeemer, indwelling Spirit of Obedience!

* In *The Structure of the Divine Society* (Lutterworth Press, 1951).